A Walk in Bardo

I lie a long, holy night, swaddled in layers of linen, eyes
coin-closed, reading
by foxfire-light the book
I am written to be.

Final chapter, there will come fire of
Easter lamb. I shall be morseled
and strewn. From which
will come feasting.

No joy without hunger, without taste, without chewing.
Without death
the master chef.

I would not go raw into the ground.

I would be eaten cooked, dressed in the most various and
brilliant spicings: cinnamon, nutmeg, cumin and turmeric
and cayenne pepper; rosemary, oregano, lemon and sea salt;
plum, ancho pepper, plantain and cranberry and ginger.

My wake a repletion, a surfeit,
consumed, nothing left over.
Not a whisker, not a nail.

Only the crowdiness of words,
ragged, regal gypsies,
hot to move on.

Cal Kinnear

Blue Begonia Press

Yakima, Washington

A Walk in Bardo
Copyright ©2008 By Cal Kinnear
Cover art envelope copyright © by John Palmer

ISBN 13: 978-0-911287-59-2
ISBN 10: 0-911287-59-0

Published by
Blue Begonia Press
225 South 15th Avenue
Yakima, WA 98902-3821
www.bluebegoniapress.com

Envoi

November again. Two years gone by. This book done now,
this walk. It is a divided and vertiginous moment. Deep
familiarity and leave-taking. But a pull, too, to leave again
at your side, all still to traverse, this house of spirits.

I've been showing Jim Bodeen poems for years. They've
hung on his poetry pole. Two years ago, I showed him a
long prose poem, forerunner to this one. He liked it.
He said, That brings in all of you! And with that whisper
of spurring, I began this work.

Just at that time I met a woman, Jennifer Johnson, who has
come this Bardo way with me, from whom I go on learning
the rich and tangling ways of Eros.

A lifetime ago as I began to waken to life, I found I had a
cousin, my mother's sister's son, John Palmer, who has
proven kindred in spirit as well as blood. We have teased
and tormented and delighted each other for years beyond
count. For the last ten years or so Jack's correspondence has
come to me in envelopes tattooed with the most remarkable
works of decoupage. They are brimming with the spirit of
Bardo, and one of these has found its way to the cover of
this book, so adroitly mortised together by a new friend,
Dan Baker. I would never have found the precise layout of
this book, which had been teasing and tormenting me,
without the good eye of another new friend, Petyr Beck.
He saw that razor margin down the center of each page
which had been just eluding me. And finally there is the
script 'Bardo' in Tibetan, from the great cyberhoard, and
Trausti. When I showed Rigzin Tingkhye this word, asked
if this indeed said 'Bardo,' he said 'Yes, Bardo.' 'Intermission,'
he said. So Bardo is 'intermission' as well!

To others I owe hours of the most delicious conversation, in-
telligent, spirited, wicked, laughing, contrarious: Lee Bassett,
Brenda Howald, Misti Uptain, Diane Sepanski, Marcos
Carmona, Mercedes Lawry, Carla Pryne, Russ Lockhart,
Susan Scott. (And not to forget weekends of solitude spent
in Lee's cabin at the confluence where the Tye River and
Beckler Creek become the Skykomish River. Where I worked
on my own writing, explored Lee's library and collection of
films, and felt with such force the sense of spending time as
double and shadow of an other, and what that has to do
with friendship.

At a little more distance, grandparents, parents, aunts, uncles,
cousins, brother, daughter, grandchildren, and all the old
friends and loves: the whole quick houseful of shades.

This is about gratitude, and more. It is to
acknowledge the force of Eros in my life, how I have been
drawn and driven, never certain of direction, never wanting
to be certain, only certain I needed at best to be giving
myself to that bittersweet force which governs.

Never losing sight on this way, in this going forth (if it can
even properly be called sight) of death, the dark imminence,
the old rampant, looming bear, the chandler of dreams.

I'm lighting up themes for you here. You'll find them again
along your way. Lace up your boots. Set out.

At Trailhead

An idiosyncratic trek (fragile mortal self, the *idios* of the Greeks, root of idiot as well, and its container, from *kratein* to contain, *krater,* a bowl to hold wine, my own vintage), untrustworthy, improper, uncivil, ignorant, fond, mutable, ephemeral.

Burning, burning, burning. This is the Buddha's vision of human life. It is a vision that wishes to be done with life, to be done with burning. The burning is true. It is not to be ignored or discounted. We burn through our lives. We may not reserve ourselves for something else. We try at risk of life to burn more quietly, to save up the modicum of fuel for a later day. We have our one flame to mingle with, to ride. This is the pleasure principle.

Many writers understand writing—poetry, novels—as a life-related career. It is far more ambiguous than that. Poetry for all its intensity and passion is close companion of death. We need a better understanding of death than we have. Poetry's backstage is Bardo.

I am a dead man walking. Where do you suppose life comes from? This famous cycle of life and death we're taught about. It's not just out there in the passage of seasons we watch and suffer. It's right here every moment. To be alive and dead. To be doubled. It is the way of the writer.

Bardo, an unsettling alien name for what we might
understand as Hades if we had not discounted such
places far back in our Christian centuries. Hades, the
shade, the dark one, the undoer.

*Sometimes the entry is a narrow door at the
bottom of a stairway. But sometimes I step
out into the brightly-lit bowl of an amphitheater.*

Bardo is earliest, and latest, and sempiternal:
('space-2' is something like the Tibetan etymology)
the space between (life and life? death and birth?).

Bardo is intermission,
the space/time of intermission,
while the play of history is on hold.

First steps

This autumn I am seeing more sharply: the indelible red of an autumn maple, hawthorn sapling with a lofted pair of late leaves, clusters of 3 or 4 red hawthorn berries, an old car on blocks, a piece of weathered and mossed fencing, a tall shingled house accented in violet and lime, pottery cats gaze down from the balconies. Yes, with the years seeing grows more subtle from long use, and more available from diminished need. And I also begin to touch on a ceaseless activity within the commonplace, substantial world, a life that is half-presence, half-something-else on which presence rests. What I begin to see is the something-else.

With age, memory sharpens in a certain way. A face, a barn, a dawn on a sea coast, a heron, a friend's way of laughing, a flying raptor-fox from a dream. These are my Images. They appear in my mind's eye. They go and return. How can they be utterly idiosyncratic? To each of us, singularly, an *idios*?

The Greek root 'idio-' has to do with the isolated self, what I will call '*idios*.' Herakleitos wrote 'One and common the world of wakers. Sleepers turn away each into an *idion*.' *Idios* is not the same as ego. Ego has much more to do with the world 'we' live in in common.

There are two boroughs of life. They are thoroughly discontinuous, they mark a difference. Waking and sleeping. The common and the utterly personal.

'A Walk in Bardo.' I woke this morning, November 12,
with those words, knowing, that's what this is, this
veer I've just taken that's begun this writing. The
twins' birthday, November 1. Full moon November
14 or 15, and just before, a week of fog. Middle of
Scorpio, my moon, my memory, my Bardo. I think
just about anything can walk in right now. Forgetfulness
and confusion yesterday morning, emotionally a little
labile, but that's the veer going on, taking its own way.

Small blind
black bird on black
stone
snake,
oh wrapped in
singing.
Night-nursed,
he invents
the infinite luminous cal-
ligrams
of moonshine
breaking the sea
to ecstatic
foam.

I have nothing else but my Images, my *idios*, to take
with me from life into Bardo, least of all this perse-
verative 'I.' Each night's dreaming tells me that. There
are images in an energetic, mobile field, and I am one
among them, losing hold.

There are no sharp edges. This is the thing we cannot
see, ego-chitonous as we are. We never leave Bardo,
awake or asleep. Consciousness is the peculiarity, the
aberration. There is a next place after consciousness.

Will there be a lesson to learn? I think that's what my
mother wanted to know, when she asked me, shortly
before she died: What did I think would come after?
Bardo. No, not lessons. No one there to learn them.
The stuff of dreams without the dreamer. Not an
empty room waiting for a party. The party always
there, to which everyone sooner or later comes. The
something-else presence rests on.

Sleep god
bear in winter
dreaming off its fat.

She was a little afraid, I think, my mother, the way she
would have been, introduced into a company of
strangers who wore unusual clothes, used large ges-
tures, spoke languages. It's a long dream, only with no
time there's no measure of length, I told her, where
you meet family and friends, and are reintroduced to
everyone you never knew. You become available to the
company of dreams. You are dream-available, it's a
lovely, frightful sort of irresponsibility. Before the re-
turn. Only, who returns?

My mother slipped into her bed like
a fine linen jacket into a box lined

   with kelp-green tissue and attar of rose
   one night, put down her book

open to a certain page, and
wandered away, an insomniac, a nightwalker now,

   gone into the strangely muraled
   bardo corridors of sleep. Where

I have seen her again,
surely.

Like singularity, I can't say what memory is. But I
know. It must be here first and before. Because mem-
ory recognizes, unerringly if we let it, recognizes with
desire. What kind of memory would that be, an infi-
nite storehouse, like Borges' Library of Babel, search-
able—to the exact scent of a madelaine, to a lost box
of letters—by the swiftness of desire?

Again, the two strands, the deep, starless night of in-
stinct, and the moon-day of memory and awareness,
harmonize with and confirm one another. A deer
stands in the edge of the woods at dawn, vanishing as
I watch. Moon-down melted into itself.

No lessons then, but messages, about what this is, this
whole business, this something else upon which pres-
ence rests. Don't listen to what I say, these words. But
listen. I love birds, their airy swiftness, their fierceness,
how they fling themselves, let themselves be torn by
torrential winds, rise, soar, watch for fish a hundred
feet below. I don't love angels with their prêt-à-porter
wings like vestments put on for a beatification,
mounting and descending the grand escalier mutter-
ing their sunlit psalms. The messengers are downstairs
in basements, in caverns and canyons, even in train
stations and airports, a little envious of us still-
breathing, a little mocking, a little (without letting it
show) frightened, for us all in this indecipherable
venture. So should we each be.

The fields of Bardo

I dreamt I was moving swiftly, skimming on the sur-
face of a broad grassland, a savannah. I looked up and
saw, in a clear sky, a great gust of wind gathering to
blow. For a moment I was afraid, of the force, until it
reached, and was a breath, joy, elation. I went on. I
saw large, tawny-gold cats in twos and threes moving
languid, without haste. One had a few black spots and
I called it leopard. Others had only shadings of
tawny-gold.

> *Smallest bird, startle-feathered.*
> *Painted bird, drawn white*
> *out of a wash of auroral purple.*
> *Seen bird of night spirit seeing.*

> *Light.*
> *Face of calmest*
> *astonishment.*
> *Light-struck.*

Borders. Whole worlds dancing into and out of focus
with one another. Poetry, on the border of communal
experience and the *idios*. Poetry, on that other border
with Bardo.

Irresponsible, yes, that's what I said. This is a strange
region where reflection, and animal nature or instinct,
reach a sort of simultaneous presence as if transpar-
ent to one another. Responsibility is the reflective
mind guiding a will, moving a body according to a
thought. In Bardo, in dream, is only the simulacrum
of a body, and reflection can find no will. But there is
movement, and it seems to be driven from everywhere,
from within, from round about, and take in walls and
cars as well as hands and hair. Instinct here is not
dark, overwhelming, hidden, it is the stuff of the im-
ages reflected-on, the life within what seeing sees. The
something-else presence rests on.

I am no scholar, have eyes
Silver-slashed black as
November rain.

I dream
broad-waking.

Eros
is a hidden and
devious master,

moonlit
scorpion.

We believe ourselves quit of faith. There are no holy
stones anymore, no miraculous statues of the Black
Virgin, no omphalic cave in a certain hill in the vast
Australian interior desert. There is only *idios* and
world. There are still borders, messages. And what do
we make of what comes our way out of mystery on
the way to mystery?

Eros

In the history of the gods, Eros seems to appear late.
'Appear' means arrive in our awareness, take an
epithet, a name. Earliest were the goddesses, who
attracted, who bore, who kept life driving. Then the
king, the warrior, the wise, even the clever, before we
ever saw the one who is each of us without face,
driven from within. 'It,' Freud called him, the blank
euphemism, before ever daring to gaze where the face
might appear. That one in the dark all limb-tangled with
Psyche, who would be face of her desire, if she could see.
Other of (same as) Hades, the unseen, the shadow.

Eros, jefe, riding master. Not mediator nor coordinator. He drives us into one another, and through, and past, into renewed solitude.

Eros the bitter-sweet who drives our wanting. Eros,
my personal *daimon* who drives my wanting, my need.
Eros singular and infinitely divisible, the propulsion,
the drivenness within the *idios*. And so I think fate as
if I had two eyes that see in different worlds. The
world we are born into in community and pass
through and out. And the world I (who am no one,
anyone) never stop dreaming. Eros the idiosyncrat;
Eros the binder. Fate, the coat of our visible colors;
fate, the hair shirt under the skin. What do I know of
what they know of how they are (inter) woven?

Eros is here in this world, torquing, driving the scene. Eros the fugitive. Eros the complicator, driving *idios* through *idios*.

The body acts out, powerful and mute. It hides and prowls, loves and fears. Poetry is a sudden discharge, a lightning (or darkening) stroke, the traces, the burn, left along the scar of passage. Poetic language has its own power in secret and distant league with the body, about which the ego knows little.

Orpheus= Morpheus

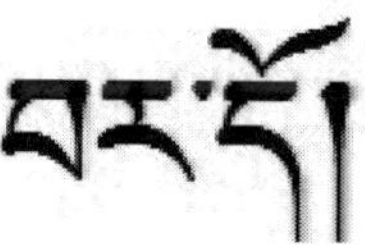

Eros in Bardo

By all accounts we have, life, blood, passion are miss-
ing from Bardo, what brings the dead thirsting to a
bowl of blood. Eros seems absent. Herakleitos says
Hades and Dionysos are the same. I say Hades and
Eros are the same, and I mean the same by it. In
Bardo, Eros the riding master does not burn in the
blood nor along the muscles. There is not any ego to
drive with obsession. Hades is the dark and the night,
and drives his currents and all the shades who live
there. He is the night landscape, shaping and shifting
and unshaping.

In dream, in Bardo, Hades/Eros is 'who is there,' the
unseen, the night just before the moment of lightning
of which Herakleitos writes: 'All these things the
lightning steers' *(Tade panta oiakizei keraunos)*. What
steers, not an old king on a throne or leaning over the
edge of a cloud to look down from immense distance,
but what tears through with sudden brilliance and is
then gone. Bardo-wisdom, what-is-not in its potential,
potent splendor. What is half-presence, half-some-
thing-else on which presence rests, mobile, passerine.

Unimaginable
touch, soft as
flight-
feather of a crane,
lightning
in its unexpected
sudden leaving

Hell

The Christian Hell is a furnace, full of fire. The figures we meet are still individuals, have not shed their names and egos, have not dissolved. They are no less driven, no less obsessive, than they were in life. Only, they are incapable—remembering and without hope. And Satan is the ultimate of Personhood. There is no death in this Hell. It is the ultimate marmoreal, memorial mausoleum.

Dante, in his *Inferno*, did not bring us to Bardo. Grotesque as the world he leads us through is, it remains the world of ego and history, with the obsession and compulsion of ethos. We have to go to Kafka, to Garcia Màrquez, to Borges, to experience something like Bardo.

The shadows of Hades are mobile. Hades is perpetually transformative. We sleepers are schooled there every night: our provenance, our destination.

The only thing Bardo has to learn from the living,
that it does not already and always have, is touch and
emotion. The substance of the body that shades can-
not have. The mysterious juncture, the ambiguous
umbilicus between living and dead.

Understand clearly. There is no hope in Bardo, be-
cause no time, no one to hope. Hope may flow into
us from Bardo, a kind of balm, but only by way of
chance.

The reports have it wrong that entering Bardo, we
leave behind the energy of life. We leave our experi-
ence of life as "I" behind. Think in terms of the un-
certainty principle— used to gathered personhood,
we miss the condensed energy, which runs everywhere,
uninhibited. Eros runs there as in life. Bardo is the
ground of Memory, eternal, alive, Eros-driven.
Memory is fluid and forward, is prospective.

Memory

Western Thought, along about the 17th Century, in order to free man from the innate and too near presence and tutelage of God, invented an empty man who needed, like a wine bottle, to be filled. A child came into the world empty. Each generation in its passing undertook the duty to fill up the next. The filling was pumped in, obsessively. What was pumped in was memory. Memory was the scratching on the blank slate. We are witnessing in our schools today a failure, a dessication of this memory.

There always was another memory. A man is a *krater*, filled with his own vintage.

There is no time before image. Image is itself and full-grown from earliest. So the two tangled senses of memory: *Memoria*, the fund of image, and the conscious capacity to retain and replay image.

Memory, in two strands: the deep, starless
night of instinct, and the moon-day of this other
memory and awareness, which harmonize with and
confirm one another.

A memory based on metaphor. Simile claims things
are like one another. Metaphor experiences that things
do like one another, want to be closer, want to ex-
change being with one another. We remember because
things love (and hate) one another, and we are in the
center of that, and experience it.

Herakleitos captures the wisdom of this memory in a
wild flower straight from Bardo: 'Aion, a child playing
at dice. The child is lord.' *(Aion pais esti paizon,
pesseuon; paidos he basileie)* 'Aion,' who is 'ages and
ages' impersoned, 'Eternity,' maybe. But not grown old
in all that time: a child. And playing at a game of
chance. The Herakleitean word *'idios'* isn't here, but
the behavior, the thinking, is. This is about a wisdom
that has more to do with chance and play than with
experience and saving up.

Twins

Twins. Two young women, born under the sign of Scorpio. (my birth moon in Scorpio) Memory-recognized, with desire. I knew them before I knew them, this is the way the mythic installs itself. Indistinguishable from the real. And everything since has changed. I can tell them from one another now, easily. There is nevertheless an identity in the something-else. I never lose sight of that. That is the wonder, and it makes other things wonderful. They are neither sisters nor lovers. The figure of some constellation has changed.

Twins: the one who comes a step behind, the dark, maybe the troublemaker, the shadow to the golden. The golden steps forward speaking, the black shadows behind, watchful, holding her silence. Each says the other, no secrets possible. This golden-and-black is a game they play with each other and the world. It will change. Will the roles, too, change? And still there is identity.

I have known them now nearly a year, these twins, celebrated their Scorpio birthday, and I was slow, a month it took before it reached me that they were born on All Souls Day, the bright day following the dark night of the dead, Halloween, Walpurgisnacht.

There is identity. There is only meant to be one at
one time, is only space for one. So fate is oddly torn.
(why perhaps with Leda's twin sons, Castor and Poly-
deuces, one was slain, the other, son of Zeus, immor-
tal; why Jacob deceived Esau of his birthright).

It is a tangle and a puzzle. It has no single meaning.
The light changes as the figure moves.

The twins set the problem of one, of *idios* brooding.
There is only space for one dreamer. What a tangled
web we weave, dream warped with dream.

So doubling in Bardo is not the same as doubling in
Reality. The brothers fight to the death in reality:
Joyce's Shem and Shaun and all their avatars. Only
room for one Father. Only room for one Reality, but
many *idion* Bardos. Enigma at the mirror-border.

And when Bardo-doubling lights like a torch, looms
through into—Reality?

Freud

Hermes shape-shifter and Eros the bull drover, we're
so close to Freud.

The life of water, its consistency and dynamic, has
created all the forms of the creatures that live in it.
The energy-night of the unconscious, the life of
darkness, has in like wise created the energy-forms of
the creatures which live in light.

One of Them (the '*athanatoi*'—how shall we say that
in English, 'deathless'? 'undead'?) came to me one
morning on the border of sleep, a woman named
Fre(u)d, and oh she had much to say, yes she spoke,
and I don't remember a word of it, and I went
through a door with her, and she showed me her
'warehouse,' a vast empty space, full of rectangles of
shadow set in deeper shadow. A space waiting to be
animated, a space potent with shades. Where she and
whoever else might appear would be just that, appar-
ent, but not therefore false. She was an articulation, a
point of focus and meeting between our worlds. She
was the plenum of that warehouse. Who there, meet-
ing her? Stored, Memory.

To recover in the outer world the lost or repressed
inner: the first, even the before. This coming here is,
remember, return, after the Bardo time, dreamer
among dreamers, washed in it all. It is never formless
(that warehouse, charged with potential), it is night the
great-rooted tree, holding its small, still-sheathed buds
of light. All of which is insisting on Freud, is it not?

Freud, for whom pleasure was the deepest grounding
principle. (Eros the bull drover.) Think of the enigma:
Freud, somber, stoic, physically reserved, with his end-
less cigars, and the pain of his cancer. So we can't
mean anything superficial and conventional by
pleasure. We do point to what drives life and the
body/mind: that energy. It's the way Lou von Salomé
was always looking: 'In the harshness and drought of
our wandering through life, however far it leads in di-
vergent ways, our thirst is slaked from the same
spring,—as the animals of the desert meet at the edge
of the same oasis at dawn or dusk.'

Repression and sublimation are what we do to our-
selves (generation after generation) to save ourselves
from ourselves (the spirit of old Hobbes looms). To
save: to spare, to put aside, in a bank—for when? But
repression doesn't save us from ourselves. We can't be
saved. We can only go there, to the source. We can
only spend. And if it's too much, well, occasionally it
is too much.

I would not do without the Marquis de Sade, not
without Antonin Artaud, not without Catherine the
Great, not without Anaïs Nin, not without Simone
Weil. Lou speaks too of: '[a way of being] whose
neediness and whose radiance don't let themselves be
artificially separated from one another, because we
ourselves are in both.'

Sexuality is there at the center, it has to be. And con-
sciousness has to be there or something like it, though
not what education has splinted and bandaged us
with. Not the poor, sorry, Ego. The counter-awareness
to the experience of Reality, the light-seep from bone
up through tissue to the skin that is natally given.

And somehow, for all that Bardo seems to be about a
taking leave of our time in body, it has everything to
do with pleasure. We go there to be washed, to be
scoured in it. To be readied. Maybe to laugh.

We never leave Bardo, awake or asleep. Consciousness
is the peculiarity, the aberration. There is a next way,
a something-like-it, after consciousness as we live in it
now.

Again, the two strands, the deep, starless night of in-
stinct, and the moon-day of memory and awareness,
harmonize and confirm one another. A deer stands in
the edge of the woods at dawn, vanishing as I watch.
Moon-down melted into itself.

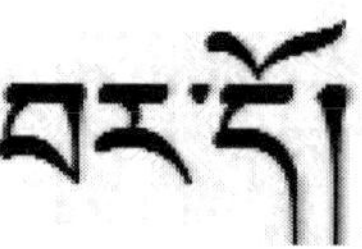

Ethos: We, the collective

We: the collective, the enduring. The inner force of
ethos. We have to understand, and we do, what the
signs, emblems, the postures and gestures, the clothing
and uniforms, the accents, jargons and slangs all sig-
nify. They make the outward and common sign of de-
sires otherwise inward and hidden. They make proud
and grand what otherwise would be shy and even
shameful. The Emperor's New Clothes makes
a parable of the unveiling that is analysis.

The dynamic of The Emperor's New Clothes. Ethos
is our air, our surround. We live in it, hard to be con-
scious of it. It is for instance mother tongue (not po-
etry yet, poetry is a long way off), how we simply
wake into it, talk it, take our mark from it, wear
its inertia and slow change.

Language, that deepest of mysteries, with its two
faces, of ethos and poetry.

Young, I struggled to master it, to get it right. I had
to learn to be precise before I knew what precision
was. First the simplest things, then the whole world
of distinctions. It was breath, and the management of
breath. It was truly the air I lived in, to make con-
scious the world. And where did it come from? From
everywhere, from everyone.

From everyone. From this fact the illusion that the
child is empty, needs 'filling' by adults. A very young
child is already full of language, needs to struggle
with its particulars. Children already have language
from birth.

I have my being in ethos and am made up of it, taking
and giving back by osmosis, and am hardly aware of
it, picking up habits and tics and accents and popular
phrases, and circulating them, the way genetic continua-
tion can be seen sinking and surfacing for generations.

Language divides and aligns us. It is how we under-
stand 'we' and 'they.' 'True,' and 'false.' It also creates
and sustains the illusion of 'I' which is not to be
confused with *idios*.

*And poetry. Poetry is a place on the border of com-
munal experience and the idios. There is a small,
brown, long-legged spider there. The spider is guard,
checkpoint and passport. Going either way. But once
there, there is no going. I have been there with it, and
I say it. Two experiences tremble into one focus.*

Ethos *daimon*

Not just passive and a medium though, ethos is a *daimon* as well. Is one stream of Eros. Is a force in the life of every psyche. It is the force that binds us among one another. It works through every one of our identifications. Even the most 'objective' and skeptical is emotionally bound with others like himself. Even though they be 'imaginary,' or dead.

The father and upright man who accepts whatever rearing and education is his lot, who earns a sufficient living, who earns a good name, who breeds and raises in turn his own family, who makes the city a stable place to live, who respects friends and enemies alike (do you know him?): he is agent of Ethos.

And the narcissistic sociopath who knows the ways, unhindered by his attachments, who seeks and claims the mayoralty, the governorship, the presidency: He is the Arch Regent of Ethos, He knows how to play the whole intricacy of strings among us.

There is the Capitol at one end of the Mall.
There is the Lincoln Memorial.
And there, sunken and scarcely visible, is
Maia Lin's Vietnam Memorial.
Fierce transmitters of ethos.

What does ethos have to do with Bardo? Ethos is the unseen guidance system of this side, of life in society. And what guides? It is the linger on things, the psychic residue, the leak from Bardo and sleep glowing here like a faint phosphorescence. What makes things image. This chair is not just a chair, holds hours of reading and thought, lacks all innocence, is drenched in a history of books. And here in my kitchen drawer is a small, tarnished silver crab fork. Setting it out on the table alongside a soup plate of clams, I think how a history of my family's meal times lies embedded in that tarnish, and the story of their times, their own parents, their friends, my father's career, and my own. The things that hold ethos only seem to lie still, the grip on us as firm as any corset lacing.

The world of the fathers and mothers, to the farthest reaches of generations, lingers with as fierce and embracing a presence as any book standing silent on a shelf. That earlier world is become invisible, but lives nevertheless all about us, and works its force. However we want to name it, or refer to it, this other, this was, is here, a piece of the half-presence, half-something-else on which presence rests.

Ethos. Brotherhoods, fraternities, societies. Father's and sons. Universities. Education, and how we pass on what is passed on, and I don't just mean knowledge. It is all about what is here, in reality, in this life, what is transmitted, what remains here, and transmutes. It has to do with what seems most living in life. The substance of ethos is seeming (the Emperor's new clothes...).

Pageant, how we display—a major feature of ethos.
No allowance in pageant for weakness, hurt, fear—the
psychological elements—though certainly for punish-
ment, disgrace, death as well as honor and acclaim. In
pageant is no protection against ourselves, no place at
all for *idios*. Here is the large, the miraculous, the
magnificent, the colorful, the melodious and harmo-
nious. In our darkest most disheveled hours we need
pageant. The cultural Self is sustainer and savior.

Ethos used to be behind doors. The family secrets.
The secrets of the firm, or the City Hall. Now it's in
the streets, on the front page, on the evening news, on
every blog on the web—celebrity, a world everted.
Ethos plays itself out in public. Fiction becomes real-
ity instantly, there is no lag time.

You know what I mean. The stock market. The NFL
and NBA. Hollywood. What bands are coming to
town this week? The school levy is failing. What are
we going to do with traffic in the city? And race rela-
tions? The newspapers and television 'cover' these
matters. But they can't be covered. They are the chan-
nels the river ethos runs in. They're 'hot.' No one
steers them. They're 'what's happening.' And who gives
directions? From what Javier María calls
'the dark back of time.'

Ethos is brutal. It does not measure the personal loss.
The loser in the basketball tournament whose life
turns sour, who drifts from one meaningless job to
another, who is arrested for spousal abuse, or robbing
a liquor store. Or he's a football star who, maybe, kills
his wife, and ends up in a Las Vegas motel, accused of
robbery and assault. The tournament and its winner
are written in the history of the game.

*Even the living, even the young, go about trailing a wake
of what they have done, what has already passed from
them into death. Which we altogether, which we
collectively tow, like a great ungainly, lumbering barge
with its own inertia, its lack of any hand at the helm.*

This is the point that divides us from animal nature.
There is in animals force, yes, aggression, yes, but in
the animal the impulse builds, discharges and recedes.
In man is imagination from the beginning, the capac-
ity, and the imperative, to hold onto image, to re-view,
to view again and again. But not with indifference.
Imagination is always erotically driven. The loop am-
plifies. Repetition builds to violence, which is some-
thing different from aggression.

*Bardo is full of strife. Where do you think we learn
it? In our dreams. Remember, it is Eros who drives it
all, the bull drover.*

Sex is everywhere in ethos. Sex, and money, rule. We can talk about money abstractly, but not about our own. About sex, we boast, we fantasize. We are mute about our own actual eroticism; it is a sinkhole into an underground torrent. It washes us back into *idios*.

Whereas heaven is an ego vision, an ultimate wish fulfillment. Heaven is a vision for ethos, a social vision, with families and choruses of the blest. Reality is desire, will, conflict.

I know from the depth of my eachness, from *idios*, that I am one, single, and at the same time all, and entire. That is an appearance, though not exactly illusion. It is life's central enigma. I am the single and only. And I am not, and can't believe it. That is from ethos, and the root of tragedy, the fuel of war.

What holds anybody to anybody anymore? 'Things fall apart. The center cannot hold.' That I feel disconnected does not mean that ethos has lost its force. It has never cared whether I understand it or not.

Ethos in the streets

What are we to make of the mobilizing of the force of ethos? The President, for instance, and the war in Iraq he and his minions (who is minion here?) have manufactured and prolong, and 'justify,' make 'right'?

What are we to make of the political response to global warming? Of course we understand ethos to be conservative, to be the way in which the voices of many generations continue to speak and have force (*mortmain*, possession by a dead hand, is not an obscure and archaic legal idea, but living in all aspects of ethos). Is ethos 'dead' weight? Is it *idios'* whisper of restraint loosed in the world and amplified, as a mere man is amplified to a king or tyrant? Ethos is deeply compulsive and holds every one of us.

In our positions and coalitions, wherever we stand, however outspokenly or passively, we are gripped in the field of ethos, a compass rose in the field of gravitation. We point, oh, we point.

Within ethos: divisions, battles joined. One of these is the individual against the state. This is a battle within ethos. *Idios* has no fight with ethos, only barely shares a world as a shadow shares what is sunlit. A dream remembered has no battle with the day. It is other. From Bardo, dream. From dream, forever, beginning.

Ethos/*idios*

Here is that enigmatic meeting point in Herakleitos' fragment I keep circling: 'One and common the world of wakers. Sleepers turn away each into an *idion*.' There are two wards of life. They are discontinuous, different, though oddly thrust through each other. Waking and sleeping. The common and the utterly personal. We navigate the difference as sleepwalkers.

A Sunday morning in the dog park in Medina, a very exclusive neighborhood of Bellevue, Washington. It's spring, the sun is bright, a gentle wind moves in the evergreen trees bordering a green, and moves in the reeds bordering a small pond. People, children, dogs, come and go from the green. A park is like money, depersonalized, bland, brushed invisibly with the ineradicable 'smell' of those who use it.

Who is surprised when another silent, apparently mild man guns down a party of barely-more-than children? They only wanted to be together with one another, accepting, dancing, hot with collective life. Every one full of dream.

Ethos may seem to nullify *idios*, banish it beyond even dream and private weeping. And still there is *idios*. Poetry is the other face of language, as if you could see the insides of words, the seeds, and the seeding within the seeds. Poetry is a place on the border marches of communal experience with the *idios*. *Idios* itself is an immeasurable, incomensurable force; what is manifest and what is working are not the same.

Tragedy:
the life *idios* drives, seen from Ethos

This life,
each dreaming,
each one the One
of an incalculable many.

Tragedy: crisis of *idios* and ethos. The crisis of the one
who has grown too large and uncontainable. The song
of Dionysos' goat slaughtered. Dionysos who is Eros.
Until crisis, the ethos wallows along.
Until the collective crisis of war.
Until the individual crisis of tragedy.

The vision that is tragedy lies deep in the Western
ethos. Greek tragedy. Shakespearean tragedy. The
plays are still with us, but we come after, and have
only the memory of an ethos in which a tragic theater
was possible.

We would be in the presence of an enormous dream
welled up out of Bardo. We would be looking at a
doubling, the Bardo-image a torch aflame, looming
through, claiming reality.

We the assembled, acknowledging what might be our
own dream stepping out into public reality. The field
of dream is not ego-consciousness. 'We' bear witness
in the presence of such an event, to the weaving (and
unweaving) of *idios* and ethos. Weaving is a crisis, a
web, a trap. Can the fabric hold?

There is an instability here, whether to speak as 'we' or 'I.' When Oedipus speaks, when Antigone or Medea, are 'we' spoken to as if to something as bound as a family? Or am 'I' spoken to from the depth of my own dreaming? This is not a question with an answer.

We face a dream acted out for the sake of us the witnesses, not for the sake of the actors. Tragic theater is not penitential. It is a display. We witnesses may be turned to stone. What we watch is pageant. In the way of dream, we understand: this is who we are.

If tragedy is not penitential, neither is it cathartic.

The social usefulness of the arts began with Aristotle's notion that tragedy was cathartic (cleansing, purging). Cleansing or purification became the point for the old city states, as later for the church. Show the people what they must avoid. Purge the *daimonic* core of *idios* for the sake of ethos. It was the 'not me,' the passover sign. The cleansing was the cleansing of a community from the taint of an overweener. Catharsis is the sign of anathema, of excommunication. Witness Oedipus at Collonus.

But the point really is: not to be rid of, but to live with the vision. The enormously energized image must be left resonate. What are the limits of *idios?* How far can ethos stretch without tearing? In these great works there is a stillness which coinhabits with the greatest possible emotion and energy. And there is no right and wrong, no lesson, not any way out.

What is the topology of our own theater? The masks
that hid the personal identity behind the dream-self
have come off. The actor seeks to disappear into the
ego-heart of his character. This theater is confessional
and penitential when colored with Christianity; it is
plaintiff when existential. With no one to respond
to the complaint.

And 'we,' chorus and auditors, we are no one, an eddy
of dusty wind, ill-defined, or defined against ourselves
in the cry of the poet: Ginsburg, Yevtushenko, Bob
Dylan, Antonin Artaud. Or 'we' are contained in the
vast sprawl of pages of our great novelists: Dostoevsky,
Tolstoy, Faulkner, Garcia Marquez, Joyce, each a great
chronicler and fabricator of what constitutes ethos.

Today's newspaper announces a new scientific discov-
ery: 'five percent of American's may have a mental
condition called intermittent explosive disorder.'
Which, these dauntless explorers note, is not at all the
same as pouting or whining. So we rename Rage. So
we muffle the great fury of Cuchulain and Achilles.
So we distance the ground in us of tragedy,
and of great joy.

Obsessive man

I remember my astonishment (mixed with distaste)
when I first read about the education of John Stuart
Mill (he was one of many; he was a model of a cer-
tain kind of education). It was an idea of education
that rested on a vision of a native child coming into
the world shapeless and void. Education filled that
void, and shaped the result with the same fierceness
the Chinese of another age applied to the shaping of
a young woman's feet. It was an idea of education that
in its turn only thinly veiled a fear of corporeal cru-
dity and barbarity and mental nullity that was under-
stood to be the alternative.

(Look at what barbarity education and science have
loosed in the world.)

Why are we so terrified of the Wild Child, unsocial-
ized, without language? An autistic child turns away,
but is by no means empty.

Bardo exists from forever, coeval, in some other di-
mension we little understand, with what we under-
stand as the universe. We ('I') come and go, never
entirely forgetting it in our waking, continuing to re-
member from our first breath till our last.

Repetition (the repetition compulsion) is in animal
nature as much as in human; that is to say, animals,
particular animals, are characterizable, typical. (They
are also idiosyncratic.)

Reason. With its forms to ensure repeatability, is
compulsive, is Freud's repetition compulsion exempli-
fied. This is reason's inner relation to mind, has noth-
ing to do with any claims against the outer.
Inner/outer is the great mystery. Right now we are in
a time when we believe that our repetitions accurately
mirror the outer. And we ignore what mirroring the
inner would lead to. But we mustn't miss
the compulsive element, and all it leads to.

Logic. Nothing must make its way into the conclu-
sion that is not in the premise. The world of logic al-
ready knows everything from before, it only needs
unfolding. This is very close to a faith. Compulsive
thinking. When I read Wittgenstein, I am nearer to
Borges, nearer to Kafka, than I am to Kant. He is so
unassuming, so attendant to the queenly logic. And
the quiver almost a smile takes a long time to reach.
The last of his propositions: "Wovon man nicht
sprechen kann, davon muss man schweigen."
(the perfect syntactical and logical balance: "What
you can't talk about , you must keep silent about."
Tautology, taken literally, so obvious a fool could
understand; taken metaphorically, the final dilemma
at the border of understanding.)

Capitol buildings represent the law, its compulsion to
be eternal and immovable. Cemetery stones and mau-
soleums represent the fixity of death as,
in our fear of it, we understand it.

Misunderstand death as rigor, as stare and grip, as the
gaze of the Gorgon before whom soul stops. The
dark whispers and sports every night. Death is alive,
has its own life. This is Bardo.

I watch Freud trying through the idea of 'infantile' to
get human nature to a state of pre-awareness, a state
that is purely body, with its streams and pools of in-
stinctive energy. I'm not sure he ever thought all the
way through the conflict between embodied, passive
mind that must be impressed (from within or with-
out, a new version of Locke, of *tabula rasa*, of what
made Mill), and mind, as he seemed to find it, that is,
never without the shape of image-in-field, dream, that
weathers sea-changes from biologic-living to Bardo.
And return. But there is an attempt at objectivity, a
'standing apart' with no footing, about Freud here, a
superiority (as if mature mind could, as if it had by
some magic this right, by some grace this sinecure) in
view of infant helplessness, just missing the *plenum*.

Freud named it 'pleasure' (*Lust*), this 'pressing toward,'
and he understood it as drive, not object. And he un-
derstood Eros. But the naming went awry. Wanting to
be scientific, he spoke of a principle, something he
could abstract, stand apart from, instead of being in
it with the urging, with Eros. And he spoke of 'It' out
of the same distancing tendency, instead of moving
close, listening to the accompanying *daimon*,
as Socrates did.

Interesting, with the theoretical formation of Ego and
Unconscious, that Freud's practice should bring to
him so many compulsives as to force it on him as one
of the grand classes of mental disorder. But of course
it is only an excess of what keeps the world running.
That was Freud's late, dark vision: analysis terminable
and interminable. The ego is its own murderous
labyrinth.

Neurosis. Freud marked it the universal reward for
this peculiar human consciousness, which is not just
animal being-awake. The beginning for all of us is in
this universal instinct, this being-awake. Have we
learned anything about the passage? There is no cor-
rection; the thing is hardwired. You would think
(many do) you could tinker with the wiring. But just
when you go to put your hand on a node, to catch
hold, here is Heisenberg back, there's nothing there,
just a likelihood, a guess at an energy and the dance it
performs as it slips away. So what do we do with it,
and the deep 'reservoirs' and our 'relations' there?

Fritz Perls entered Bardo by the dream. He felt the
unifying dynamic of everything that went on in a
dream. But he couldn't altogether let go of an ego-
centered psychology, and so treated dreams as a way
of bringing the devalued out of the closet and into
the parlor and dining room again. But in fact none of
it was ever created or spun-off by ego. Ego has always
been the thief, the pickpocket, getting away with what
it can, good *bricoleur*, to patchwork into a fine studio
portrait of itself. How readily we make fictional real-
ity in order to forget our real origins.

Brooding man

The brooding man, the dreamer,
remains outside the commons. *Idios*, each to himself,
an *isolato* as Ishmael called himself (*One and com-
mon the world of wakers. Sleepers turn away each into
an own* (*idion apostrephesthai*), says Herakleitos).

The body acts out, powerful and mute. It hides and prowls, loves and fears. Poetry is a sudden discharge, a lightning (or darkening) stroke, the traces, the burn, left along the scar of passage. Poetic language has its own power in secret and distant league with the body, about which the ego knows little.

Idios is anti-ethos. Socrates spoke of his *daimon* speaking at his shoulder. *Daimon* is variously experienced, as seducer, preceptor, invader. The particular pipeline of each to the whole, the breakout. Or break-in.

Dangerous, that period when a man or woman begins to realize that when I speak, when I say 'I think…' there is a division, someone whispers, while I speak, or write. Until the illusion of the self-directing ego shatters. I am spoken to. You might as well believe in channeling. Except you will never discover the identity of the whisperer.

The whisperer in the ear, close, intimate, with never a
face, is *daimon*. This is what it means. The whisper
that at once urges and restrains. Urges to lust, jeal-
ousy, murder, betrayal, and in the hearing of the whis-
per makes the hearer draw back, with a sudden catch
of the breath. The whisperer who is nearer than near,
close and intimate, and, as in all intimacy, shameless.

The ego, as Freud taught, may tame and deny the
whispered urge. The ego, as history teaches, may also
set aside the restraint, learn with some success how to
not listen.

Murder is born here, near and intimate as a brother.
It whispers out of a doubling darkness, which spins
with the cyclonic (and anti-cyclonic) forces of
creation and destruction.

Yes, murder, of course. Macbeth. Othello. Oedipus.
Schooled by no one but the dark
in which we are immersed.

But love too. Love is its own compulsion (Eros the bull
drover). Is at once the deepest isolation and separation
from all community, and the deepest communion.

In the brooding man, the sea coils and whispers, full of a low music, whispers of murder and passion, the sea incarnadine with Eros. Whispers in the privatest chamber of the ear, where language is not yet, or no longer. Only a whisper, only a kiss. Alone.

The brooding man, the dreamer. Brood, from breed, proliferating. The mind with itself in dark, hen on a warm nest, the whole quiet space of that, dream and the world turning back to dream, all that color and touch and motion and song.

The brooding man lives at the confluence of *daimon* and ethos; we come back to that so-central fragment of Herakleitos: *Ethos anthropoi daimon.* The *daimon* a whisperer of desire and restraint, a single split voice, intimate. Sometimes immediate as a touch on the shoulder, sometimes large as a winter ocean storm. Choice has no place here. This is why the word 'fate' appears. No two hear the same whisper, and yet the whisper is from Bardo. What I hear gives me my features, my rhythm, my voice. I am wood with a certain grain, a shape to be carved out, a fracture plane.

(Ethos whispers too, faint from the skin of reality. May be, it's the same whisper. Nothing to do with conscious mind here.)

If the whisper gets too insistent, too loud, it will
break out, others will notice. They will
let you know.

If the whisper gets too insistent, you may find it too
much, may need to shutter. Work. Worry. Think.
Good obsessive, rational thought. Stay busy. Drink,
do drugs. You can almost shut it up. It goes on, a leak
in the roof, a mouse in the attic, a night wind against
the window, the obsessive tedious tune you can't
forget: "Blue Moon," "The More We Get Together."

What suddenly does fall through, filling the world—a
morning of snow; a lover, gone.

This one, this underworld Eros, this whisperer. He
does not lie burrowed down in some inverted aerie.
He makes dream, dream is his whisper. Whisper is
word, whisper is tone, whisper is shade.

I hear whispering, wake to the fading mist of dreams.
How shall we imagine a whisperer, this horseman, this
bull drover, this slash of lightning?

He is not objective, is the stuff and genius of *idios.*
We founder on our God-ideas here. I experience pres-
ence and person, but not ego or body or locus. Hades
the disjoiner, the dissolver; Eros the weaver and knotter.
At once, in one.

He drives me with his whispering which I can no way
sort from what I call my own voice.

In our enlightened time, we have learned to discount
the urge to personalize the unknowable. But we know
ourselves as personed, understand action, will, pattern,
consequence only from a perspective of personhood.

How can this unperson, this Eros, be so intimate, un-
derstand me so in his whispering, and yet be no plan-
ner, no schemer, or fater, or designer? Be in fact, as
Emily Dickinson understood, indifferent?

How, in my brooding on all this, could I come, living,
to know myself as unpersoned, in order better to be
known by what seems to know?

Lou Andreas Salomé noted that the work of art itself,
in its aesthetic specialization, is beside the point.
It takes hold of, laughingly strips out the artist, leaves
him in one way or another burned. The real art is
played out in the *barrios* of Bardo, where a life (*idios*,
fate, character, *daimon*, crossroads, Eros), my life, of
which I can never become wholly 'conscious' (but
aware in other ways and how to find the ways to re-
port those), is the real work. This is where she is
Freud's weird sister.

There never was Oedipus. Oedipus is from Bardo. Never was Odysseus, never was Macbeth. Perhaps the name from some once-ago, and a mist of story, itself already the whisper from Bardo. Presences who entered by the ear. Heard-of beings, not anyone ever met. At a real crossroads, for instance. Heard by Sophocles, by the blind Homer, himself a shade heard of. Heard by Shakespeare. Heard from the whispering in their ears.

There is an ancient myth of an ancestor who is hermaphroditic. Man and woman undivided. In division, in passion, we struggle back toward that unity. That fantasy is alive in some recess of my imagination. I have imagined a sister, my twin, in some Before, some Other, who has never reached Reality, except as she glimmers through the flesh of the women I have loved.

The twinned man

Not long ago, I walked in my sleep, two nights running—in a dialogue with my twin who wished to remind me of his presence and his rights. He the dark one, so easily forgotten, the one who falls down, but not out of clumsiness—because he is the one who possesses weight, who fulfills gravity, who reminds me of sleep, and the far edge of dream.

This dark one is what Caliban means.

In a dense, dark moment of 'sleepwalking' we two met and struggled. Or, he, for that time, usurped me. Or, he, for a brief space, escaped the prison which for him 'I' am.

The previous night, 'I' had mis-set my alarm. It went
off at midnight. I turned it off and went back to
sleep. The mistake should have been a warning.

This night, 'I' get up very close to that
same midnight, as if remembering. He turns on
lights. He shaves. He does not shower. He puts on my
usual sweat pants, sweater, wool socks. He turns the
heat up as I always do. He puts water in the tea kettle.
He puts it on the burner, and turns it on. I always
begin my morning with tea. He goes to the front door
to look for the morning paper, which is not there. I
notice the time, not time yet to be up, and go back to
bed. In the morning when 'I' wake, the dry, very hot
kettle still sits on the burner. It has not welded to the
burner. I take it out and put it in the back yard to
cool in the night rain. We are lucky. This has been a
crisis of two, we have not come to the end of it, no
one owns it.

And how? Responsibility is a pointing finger in the
waking world. Mother, you see?
Bardo is not about responsibility.

One night later, 'I' 'wake' (language comes to its limits
here, can't quite cope) in front of the bathroom mir-
ror, lights on (who turned them on?), a cut over my
left eyebrow bleeding heavily. I have a vague memory
of a struggle with the shower curtain. Beyond that I
remember nothing. At first I think I have fainted; but
the lights, I never turn on the lights when I get up in
the night. He has turned on the lights.

Who was it got me there? Who blundered blindly for-
ward and fell? And to what end? There is place for
one, not two. Is this a struggle for control? And what
would sleep do, control won?

I am cutting vegetables, preparing dinner. The knife
escapes my hand, rebounds from the cutting board,
turns over in the air as my hand tracks it, misses, the
knife hits point first into the floor. I shout out loud
at myself in a rage against my clumsiness. He is here,
mute, submissive, treacherous. I have watched skilled
chefs cut themselves, just so. We are so close, he with-
out feature. He is inseparable from my balance, my
dexterity, my timing. It is easy to find him not simply
stupid and clumsy, to find him intentionally sinister.

I remember how I have thought of my twin friends:
the one I have noticed coming a step behind, the dark,
maybe the troublemaker, the shadow to the golden.
How each says the other, no secrets possible. This
two-in-one is a game they play with each other and
the world. And I remember how two experiences
tremble into one focus.

One among the enigmas of *idios*
in this world.

The traitor

I've been reading John LeCarre for so many years, since my youth. Of course the excitement, the suspense, the mystery. But a deeper thing than that. It is the question of betrayal, what it is, where it comes from. Secret betrayal, which 'turns its coat,' seems still to fly all the colors and manners of ethos—of who we are born and raised—but gives, deeply and secretly, the lie to it all.

The traitor follows unlit ways, is a dark one, an undoer of light, shape, order. His is an inner conflict before it is an outer history, a being divided against himself. A man twinned, following himself, whispering in his own ear. But who is the whisperer and why do I trust him?

Richard Meinertzhagen, British soldier, spy for his country, and birder, has recently been discovered to have been a great betrayer of Truth and Science. He worked as a spy during World War I. Through carefully built 'disinformation' he had a hand in British victory against the Turks in the Middle East. He might have served as a model British gentleman.

Meinertzhagen knew and served with T.E. Lawrence. He wrote journals lifelong, which he forged and altered (think of placing conscious lies in your own journal). He was a well-known collector of bird specimens, and wrote books on rare birds in Asia. It turns out he stole bird skins from the collections of others, claimed them as his own trophies, and reassigned their provenance. He was a scientist and a betrayer of science. He was an honored and upright man, and a devious man. He may have murdered his wife and created a lie to secrete it. There is compulsion. There is division. There is no explanation.

It would seem that fiction, the creation of which is betrayal's first step, is in the measure of ethos a perilous business, and deeply rooted in the human soul.

Thinly veiled, it is the story of God (self-)betrayed by his wisest, truest angel, Satan. Before the division became sacred history it was merely what it is: a division awareness experiences at whatever price of ignoring. There seems to be no beginning to division.

Or we may see it as Eros himself self-divided in his avatar as Ethos, the one who binds cities and nations, crossed by Eros as *daimon/idios*, the dark force streaming out from dream. We need to feel the intimate commingling of these forces, what the whisper of betrayal feels like, what it is about. And maybe why the image of the Confidence Man figured so often and prominently in 20th Century literature.

<h1 style="text-align:center">Postscript</h1>

We won't ever know, will we?

The sun was in Taurus at my birth. I am earth and weight. What I step on, I trust, as far as it will bear my weight.

My moon sign is Scorpio, I am *ankylometis*, devious minded, I speculate by the light of a candle about what is deep and hidden.

We have in evolution modified by ecology an idea of how life recycles itself, deeply economical, reusing matter and form, playing, varying. We understand how death is inherent to change and cycling. The thought of evolution was born of skeptical, scientific minds in an age of skepticism, in strong measure atheist, even anti-religious. Even the great soul-thinker Freud could not escape materialism. Even Jung could not escape a measure of scientism. Suppose (without reverting to religion) the laws of soul enact the same recycling, the same economy, the same dissolution and reformation, the same playfulness?

At the end of individual existence we each
dissolve into a collective psyche, are stirred about, and
a measure of the stuff poured into a new mould: a
hard thought for a self that has used its life to make
something special of itself. The question we are left
with then—what is the point of 'here'? What does
this ego-enterprise, this death-concluded narrows,
matter? Well, ethos remains, coming into the presence
of which is for each new life the opening of the soul
to the speaking ancestors, the works, from the Las-
caux animals to a Fellini film. To Memory. Returning,
we meet ourselves, in wonderment.

In consciousness we create complexities out of mate-
rials that well up from sleep, nearest relatives to the
outer world, which we call Reality and which we seem
to govern. We give these complexities of day back to
Bardo. In Bardo the recombinations take place that are
the dreaming equivalent of genetic evolution in
physis. *Pace* the great religions, through all this we be-
come neither more spiritual nor more evil. The dream,
as in *Finnegans Wake*, while remaining the same and
One, becomes, generation after generation, both
wilder and more intricate.

In Bardo (with those we think of as the dead,
the spirits) are the lost animals, the ruins and ravages
of the land, and also the landscapes of an earth made
new again, or as never before, wild and lovely. Eden
and Armageddon, Hiroshima, holocaust, Paradise. It
means we can make either real, in the end. They are a
part of what we know, what is written with deep
needles in our tissue. Glory and despair are a part of
the entire texture. This is timelessness. We may see,
but this is not where we live.

The two great world-dividing religions, Christianity
and Islam, share a vision of 'end' and 'afterlife.' They
'see' a radical fracture, a moment reached when the
blessed and damned are separated, World and Time
as we know them end. Kingdom come,
transfiguration, timelessness we can't now understand
loosed from Bardo.

But it will not be loosed, it belongs to Bardo. What
will happen will always happen Here. Nothing that is
not already with us and around us. And the End is
(and will be—this enigma of time/timelessness)
always in World, nowhere else (no Where else, no
u-topos). We are buried back in the mind (and the
matter) again. No one remains 'self' beyond death. I
(you/I) dissolve at death in Bardo, in the common
soul, in the dream.

We should not imagine there are now more souls liv-
ing than in, say, Plato's time. The soul stuff is merely
fractured more (don't we know that, feel diminished
by it?). The End intensifies in multitudes and in vio-
lence. Here. Always return. Here. And there is/will be
no separation of the flock. We remain matter/soul of
the same whole. Here. Toward a bitter approaching
End. Apocalypse. The dream of End awakening. But
because dream, never separable from that other End,
Paradise.

The enmity of Christian and Muslim, Jew and Mus-
lim, echoes of the original myth-time brother-hatred,
brother-murder, the slaying of Abel by Cain, eternal
events from Bardo, the soul-well, the recycling of all
that makes up the world-life of the soul and of his-
tory, repetition and variation all the way from the fur-
thest mists of memory: it is all woven into that
masterful novel, *Finnegans Wake. Ricorso* upon
ricorso down the clans, cities cultures, nations
of human history. Our dream, the cycles that
always come back
Here.

(Do we not know—is it not inscribed into history,
into every age of ethos—that 'Now' is a trial-in-the-
narrows?)

(But there are no lessons, no moral victories, and fame
is not a trophy, but a quick flare.)

And which is for the sake of which? (life for afterlife?
Or between-life to sort and ready for the new?) I will
not know, will I?

A poem is a mark, an ember, left behind, an incendi-
ary, to point what 'I' can reach to, beyond self.

All life-gain collects Here. What 'I' have come back to
from bathing in the collective psyche. It is here and all
around, in the air and sea and forests, in the paintings
and music and books. The Eternal Return of the soul
is the End, not as terror and tedium, but something
like the electric arc of sexual ecstasy and the calm of
the bodhisattva fitting one another.

Where communication would be by touch and the
grace of sound, by dance and song and poetry. Imagine!

Be easy.
It is 4:50 in the morning.
Dreams are still near.
Soon enough you will be someone again.

The end

A bear was killed the other night, a young brown bear,
in a neighborhood near the University, right in the
city. A young bear killed by the police, by civil ser-
vants, or, no, not killed exactly, frightened to death by
the harassment that reached out from their fear of
bears. Fear doing violence against fear. Isn't this the
tone of the modern city?

Going out into the city has come to feel a risk. I don't
mean I feel someone will hurt me. I mean the air is
too full of what passes, and is lost to view, and clings.
And whispers. And gestures.

Young, fear is useful.
Old, it is no longer of use,
is a hindrance.

So we have two ways: the obsessive and the brooding.
They don't exactly face off. They wear each other's
faces sometimes. Sometimes you don't know what
you're facing. It's not a matter of a new program: such
as Surrealism was, say. That's just obsession answering
obsession. It's a matter of to live in *idios*, maybe un-
noticed. And what would that be?

*I dream of my dog, dead now some five years, a
Samoyed, an irrepressible spirit, even to the end of
her nearly twenty years. I am walking her on a leash
across volcanic rock by the ocean. Her gait is un-
steady. She is old. Suddenly she slips into the water. I
am horrified and go to look. She is still connected to
me by a filament I hold in my hand. She is deep
beneath the water, swimming powerfully, her legs
spread wide. She is a polar bear, at home in the sea.
She is not looking back.*

The magnitude of the energy of the physical universe
equals the magnitude of the energy of the psychic
universe. The ego is small, frail, and at the mercy of
storms. But it opens dizzyingly on the vast.

Why does my eye and thought keep reverting to the
barbaric flower and leaf of Spring?

Nothing about Bardo means a crazed life.
Compare your dreams to your 'reality.' Exaggerations,
little variants to make you laugh, or cry, or tremble
with fear. Ego is useful while we are growing up. Then
it's time to move on. This is the difference now. I find
an awareness that doesn't worry about centers, that
weaves itself among other awarenesses.

*Huge and sudden against the backyard pine, pileated
woodpecker, ah, yes, but equally sudden the flying fox
of my dream bringing his kill to my hand where I
stand on an aerie-porch looking out over jungle.*

I take my midday walk among the remarkable flowers
of spring, in their profound and barbaric colors, and
the new red leaves, and shoots with red bark, and red,
winged seeds of the neighborhood. Each flower is an
energy expressed in pattern. Nothing I could put in
word or mathematical formula. I mean form as imme-
diate and perceptible as the individuality of a human
face. They are still, and surround me, and are alive.
This is hallucinatory and vertiginous territory.

Image (in sense or imagination) is gestalt, it is not
composite. In afterthought, anything may be taken
apart, may be understood as composed. But an image,
like a flower, like the leap of a dancer, begins from a
nothing, which is its own center, and explodes. Sci-
ence, the implacable ethos of our time, with its fan-
tasy of objectivity and abstraction, wants to have it
both ways, in motion and in stillness. Heisenberg saw
his way through that one, said No, not both ways.
DNA wants to capture origin and fate in number. But
idiosyncracy has already slipped silently loose
from number.

The old thought of *Chakra* serves us better—a dark,
formless, precisely located energy source ready to take
body/form. This is true also of how image appears in
the mind, from a precisely located nowhere.

Here, the tangle of *idios* with *daimon* and *physis* is
most intricate and dark. The translation is inaccurate
that 'character' is fate. Character is conscious, ego-
and ethos-based. *Idios-daimon-physis-ethos*, in their
precise dark knotting explode into what is fate, that
idiosyncratic gyrocompass which spins out each life.

No wizardry, no smoke and mirrors. Only the intens-
est, most various perception of what goes on, within,
and without.

I want a garden to surround me with leaf and flower,
with summer stillness and fragrance. So close there is
no path. Could I live there? Could I learn to be
simply content? It seems not. To be surrounded with
beauty will not satisfy. I know myself, I will grow
restless. Why are we not stalk and flower, simple, full
of stillness and burst? Why is it we have feet? Have
hands? This is a question from Bardo to us living.
A question, not a lesson.

In Bardo, with those we think of as the dead, the spir-
its, are the lost animals, the ruins and ravages of the
land, and also the landscapes of the earth made new
again, or as never before, wild and lovely. Eden and
Armageddon, Hiroshima, holocaust, Paradise. It
means we can make either real, in the end. They are a
part of what we know, what is written with deep
needles in our tissue. Glory and despair are a part of
the entire texture. This is the timelessness we can
never bring back.

The whisper multiplies—no longer one, close, in the
ear—becomes a house. The lights dim, a theater, cur-
tain time. A hubbub, a hush of excitement. The cur-
tain will open on the great wizard, Pro(s)per. Curtain.
No one. The great globe itself has dissolved, leaving
not a rack behind. Such stuff as dreams are made on.
All that desire, a fading dusk in a narrow space.

In a garden.

Not the lightning here. Not night. The full day of
spring. They stand around me all and close, leggy,
leafy, flower-headed. They don't stand back, on view;
they are here, present and deeper than present. For the
moment I am among them, waist high, shoulder high,
at once the youngest, gaiest children, and the most de-
lighted elders. I know I can't stay. Soon I'll be gone
away to memory and words. It's all right. They don't
leave me, they come along, they have always been here.
The Garden. We know it, you and I,
either side of death.

I do not believe in belief. Reality and dream are
equally hallucinatory. When I speak about what is
not, the half-something-else on which presence rests,
I am making no statement of faith. When I speak of
the miraculous form of a flower, I know that no
person who has ever lived could have invented one.
A flower is before any waking mind. And after.

I know that.

A flower is always just
setting out, so
young, it's not yet dawn, not even

spring, and
without a suitcase, full
of the ferocity of arrival